AMERICA'S Ben Franklin

by Steven Jay Griffel

Boston, Massachusetts
Chandler, Arizona
Glenview, Illinois
Upper Saddle River, New Jersey

Illustrations
Opener, 2, 3, 5, 8 Nathan Trewartha.

Photographs
Every effort has been made to secure permission and provide appropriate credit for photographic material. The publisher deeply regrets any omission and pledges to correct errors called to its attention in subsequent editions.

Unless otherwise acknowledged, all photographs are the property of Pearson Education, Inc.

Photo locators denoted as follows: Top (T), Center (C), Bottom (B), Left (L), Right (R), Background (Bkgd)

6 Library of Congress; 9 Library of Congress; 11 Library of Congress; 12 National Archives; 13 Library of Congress; 15 National Archives.

ISBN-13: 978-0-328-67692-7
ISBN-10: 0-328-67692-6

7 V0FL 16 15 14 13

Who Was Benjamin Franklin?

When Ben Franklin signed the Declaration of Independence, he was 70 years old. He was the oldest American to sign the Declaration. He was also, perhaps, the most famous American of his time.

Franklin's life was one of the first American success stories. He was born into a poor family, one of 17 children. Through hard work, Franklin became an inventor, scientist, and writer. He was also a famous **diplomat.** Today, we can learn a great deal from his life.

Franklin's Childhood

Many leaders of the American Revolution came from wealthy families. Ben Franklin was not one of them. Born in Boston on January 17, 1706, Franklin was the youngest son in his family. Like most boys of the time, Franklin expected to become an **apprentice**. His brothers had been apprentices, sent off from home as boys to learn a trade, such as printing.

In exchange for learning a trade, apprentices had to work for a master for several years. Some apprentices had to serve their master for ten or more years.

During Franklin's time, apprentices worked in trades such as these:

Blacksmith maker of horseshoes, nails, and tools

Shoemaker maker of shoes

Carpenter and Joiner builders who use wood

Silversmith maker of silverware and other household items

Cooper maker of casks and barrels

Wheelwright maker of wheels for wagons and carts

Becoming an Apprentice

Franklin didn't become an apprentice at first. Instead, he went to school, for which his parents had to pay. It was too expensive, so they took him out after just two years. Franklin, now ten, became his father's apprentice.

Franklin tried to teach himself. He read every book he could find. By the time he was 12, he was a skilled reader, but an unhappy apprentice. One of Franklin's brothers, James, ran a print shop. James knew that Franklin would make a great printer. Franklin signed on to be James's apprentice. Franklin, however, would have to work for James for nine years.

Franklin and his brother argued about many things. Franklin decided that he could not work for his brother any more. However, if Franklin stayed in Boston, he might be forced to keep working for his brother. So, Franklin decided to go to Philadelphia. Franklin thought he could avoid trouble in Philadelphia. Plus, he felt that he had a better chance to make something of himself there. In 1723, at age 17, Franklin secretly left Boston.

Young Ben Franklin worked as an apprentice to his father, a candle-maker.

Franklin in Philadelphia

When Franklin arrived in Philadelphia, he did not know anyone. Fortunately, he soon found work as a printer. Just a few years later, Franklin started his own print shop. Franklin worked hard at his printing business. He decided to print an almanac. These books were very popular then. They were fun and easy to read.

Franklin called his almanac *Poor Richard's Almanack*. It had stories, jokes, and wise sayings. Franklin's almanac became the most popular one in colonial America. As a result, Franklin became wealthy and well known all over the colonies. By this time, he was 42 years old, a husband, and a father. Franklin was ready to try something new.

Franklin used a fake name, Richard Saunders, for himself when he published *Poor Richard's Almanack*.

Poor Richard, 1733.

AN

Almanack

For the Year of Chriſt

1733,

Being the Firſt after LEAP YEAR:

And makes ſince the Creation	Years
By the Account of the Eastern *Greeks*	7241
By the Latin Church, when ☉ ent. ♈	6932
By the Computation of *W. W.*	5742
By the *Roman* Chronology	5682
By the *Jewish* Rabbies	5494

Wherein is contained

The Lunations, Eclipſes, Judgment of the Weather, Spring Tides, Planets Motions & mutual Aſpects, Sun and Moon's Riſing and Setting, Length of Days, Time of High Water, Fairs, Courts, and obſervable Days.

Fitted to the Latitude of Forty Degrees, and a Meridian of Five Hours Weſt from *London*, but may without ſenſible Error, ſerve all the adjacent Places, even from *Newfoundland* to *South-Carolina*.

By *RICHARD SAUNDERS*, Philom.

PHILADELPHIA:
Printed and ſold by *B. FRANKLIN*, at the New Printing-Office near the Market.

From Poor Richard's Proverbs:

- A penny saved is a penny earned.
- An ounce of prevention is worth a pound of cure.
- Eat to live, and not live to eat.
- Early to bed and early to rise, makes a man healthy, wealthy, and wise.
- The worst wheel of a cart makes the most noise.
- Fish and visitors stink after three days.
- Well done is better than well said.
- The sleeping Fox catches no poultry. Up! Up!

Franklin decided to put his skills and wealth to work, to serve his community. He felt it was his duty as a citizen to help his community. No **civic** duty was too large or too small for him. For example, Philadelphia had many muddy and dark streets. Franklin worked to get the city's streets paved and better lit.

Franklin remembered how important reading had been in his childhood. Books were still hard to come by, though. To help solve this problem, Franklin set up one of America's first libraries. He also raised money for a new hospital. Franklin even helped create the postal system we use today.

Inventor and Scientist

Franklin worked hard to come up with practical solutions to everyday problems. In his time, houses were poorly heated. Most of the heat came from fireplaces—and it went right out the chimney. People burned a lot of wood, but they still couldn't keep warm. To help solve this problem, Franklin designed a new stove. His stove needed less wood *and* it created more heat. Franklin also invented bifocals, a new type of eyeglasses.

This picture shows how an artist imagined the electricity experiment many years after it happened.

Franklin's most famous invention resulted from his experiments with electricity. The way the story is told, Franklin and his son flew a kite during a thunderstorm. A large key was tied to the end of the kite string. When the lightning hit the kite, electricity traveled down the string. When it reached the key, Franklin saw an electric spark. This proved that lightning was indeed electricity.

Most likely, Franklin did the experiment in a safer way than it has been told. If Franklin had done the experiment as described, he probably would have died.

Franklin used his experiments to invent the lightning rod. These metal rods were placed on buildings. They protected them from lightning, a major cause of fire. Franklin's inventions made him even more famous.

Public Servant

Franklin considered public service his most important civic duty. At age 50, Franklin became more active in colonial politics.

In 1764, Franklin went to Great Britain to represent the Pennsylvania colony. His political skills were put to the test. Parliament had passed the Stamp Act. This law required the colonists to buy special stamps. They had to buy the stamps for newspapers, court papers, and other documents. In effect, the Stamp Act raised taxes on the colonists.

Members of Parliament and King George III expected the colonists to obey all British laws. However, they did not let the colonists elect representatives to serve in Parliament. The colonists became very angry at this unfair treatment.

Franklin worked hard to convince the British to repeal, or end, the Stamp Act. For four hours, Franklin presented his arguments to Parliament. In the end, Parliament agreed with Franklin. It ended the Stamp Act. Franklin was now the leading voice for the Americans.

For the next few years, Franklin stayed in Britain. He worked to keep the peace between Britain and its American colonies. Parliament, however, kept passing unfair laws. Back home, the colonists kept protesting against British rule.

Colonists protesting the Stamp Act burned Stamp Act papers in Boston.

Franklin and the Fight for American Independence

In 1775, Franklin became convinced that both sides were headed for war. He returned home to America. By the time he returned home, the American Revolution had begun. Although he was nearly seventy years old, Franklin agreed to do all he could to help the colonies gain independence. He was elected as a **delegate** to the Second Continental Congress. He represented Pennsylvania at the Congress. There, he helped draft the Declaration of Independence.

If the Revolution failed, everyone who signed the Declaration of Independence could have been put to death. Franklin's signature showed how much he loved his country. Can you find his signature?

Franklin made many friends in France. These friends helped him convince the king of France to help the Americans fight the British.

Diplomat in France

By late 1776, the Americans were losing the war to the British. To win the war, the Americans needed help. Congress sent Franklin to France. His job was to persuade the French king to give the Americans money and supplies.

When Franklin arrived in France, he was already famous there. He met many important people in France. Then, he worked with his new friends to win over the French king. Franklin told the king that helping the Americans would also hurt France's enemy, the British. Franklin had convinced the king.

A Timeline of Franklin's Life

1706
Ben Franklin is born in Boston.

1723
Franklin goes to Philadelphia.

1757
Franklin goes to England.

1765
Stamp Act is passed.

1766
Stamp Act is repealed.

1775
Revolutiona
War begin

Back Home

Franklin stayed in France for about eight years. He made sure the French kept their promise to send help. Then, Franklin helped the British and Americans sign an agreement to end the war. By this time, he was nearly eighty years old and ready to return home.

The American War for Independence had been fought and won while Franklin was in France. He had not fired one shot in defense of his country. Yet, Franklin had sacrificed a great deal. For many years, he had lived far from home, helping his country from overseas. Without his efforts, America might not have been able to defeat the British.

1776
Franklin goes to France.

1776
Declaration of Independence is signed.

1783
Treaty of Paris officially ends Revolutionary War.

1785
Franklin returns to America.

1787
The U.S. Constitution is signed.

1790
Franklin dies.

After Franklin returned home, he joined delegates to write the United States Constitution. During his final years, Franklin kept working on new inventions. He also wrote newspaper articles. In 1790, only months before his death, Franklin sent a letter to the United States government asking that slavery be ended. Even until the very end of his life, Benjamin Franklin did all he could in service for his country.

From humble beginnings, Franklin rose to become one of the great American leaders of all time. His life's story still serves to inspire us.

Benj. Franklin

Glossary

apprentice a young person who agrees to work for someone for a set period of time in exchange for learning a trade or skill

civic related to being a citizen

delegate someone who represents others, such as an elected representative in government

diplomat a person who officially represents the government in its dealings with foreign governments